ADVANCE PRAISE FOR *AFFORDED PERMANENCE*

"Liam Day has set before us a nostalgic escape plan, a delirium of cartography and prismatic urban planning loosed from the Bay State, and waiting here for you like a dazed anatomy dummy. *Afforded Permanence* is far more pricey and valuable than the title suggests, and you will not regret tuning into this soundtrack of lyric transit and visitation."

— SIMEON BERRY, author of *&*

"In poems that unfold in refractive, meditative fashion, Liam Day incisively illustrates how individual stories reflect and are inextricable from those of a community. With agility and grace (attributes that are equally estimable in negotiating the MBTA), lessons are recounted then recanted, mutterings yield to utterings and routines indelibly transformed. Fueled by precision and wit, tinged with remorse, I'd gladly board any of these poems and ride them as often and as far as I can."

— RODNEY WITTWER, author of *Gone & Gone*

"*Afforded Permanence* traces select bus routes (roots) in and around Boston in poems that tell stories, evoke memories, and capture histories of the heart and mind. His speaker throughout is streetwise and tuned to the rhythms of the city, its various environs, and beyond: this is someone you want to know, both for his sense of direction and for his ways with words. These are beautifully crafted poems—formally accomplished and lyrical, with details that chart the pleasures and complexities of urban life. This is the best, most necessary kind of map."

— MARY PINARD, author of *Portal*

"These are poems which can be of use to us, in our actual lives. They take for granted that we can all manifest some kind of potent and powerful spiritual energy and are concerned with the immediate now in all its multivalent plentitude."

— NATE PRITTS, author of *Right Now More Than Ever*

AFFORDED
PERMANENCE

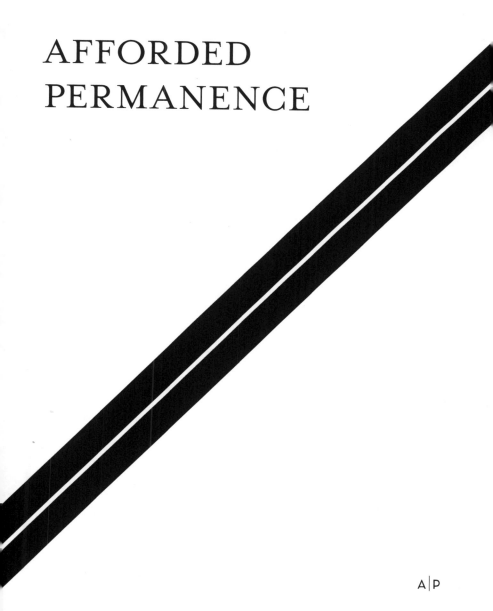

A|P

Published by Aforementioned Productions. Aforementioned and AP colophon are trademarks of Aforementioned Productions, Inc.

Poems in this collection originally appeared, some in varied form or under alternate titles, in the following publications: *apt, U.m.Ph! Prose, Wilderness House Literary Review, Slow Trains Literary Journal*, and at WGBH.org.

ISBN: 978-1-941143-01-8

Published December 2014.

Jacket design by Carissa Halston.

Front cover photo by Andre Vandal. Back cover photo courtesy of The Massachusetts Office of Travel and Tourism.

Book designed by Carissa Halston and Randolph Pfaff.

Printed in the United States of America.

aforementioned.org

AFFORDED PERMANENCE

LIAM
DAY

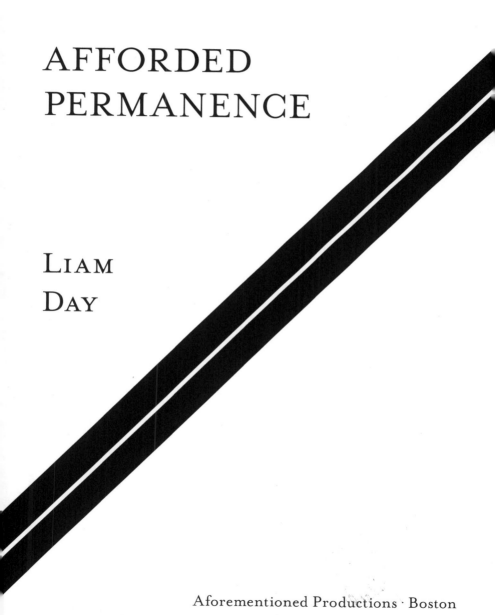

Aforementioned Productions · Boston

To my wife Nicole, who made what ensues possible, and to my parents, whose example I follow and whose dreams for me I continue to hope I will one day fulfill.

CONTENTS

THE BOY ON THE BUS

counts down the red lights. *The light,*
he says of each, *will change in three, two, one.*
If he is wrong and it doesn't, he just starts
counting again, but if he is right and the bus
slips into gear and begins to roll forward,
he turns to his mother with a triumphant look,
as if he held in his small body and high voice
the power to change traffic lights.

10 - PANOPTICON

Some routes cross the city, some circumvent it;
some, like blood vessels, work from limb
to heart and back again—
from City Point at the gate to the inner harbor
to Copley Square in the shadow of the Hancock Tower,
the slab of blue glass redolent of a tombstone.

From so many places in my life, so many places
surrounding the city like an army in siege,
I've watched its panels catch the light:
Chelsea, Somerville, West Roxbury,
the top floor of the Victorian in Dorchester,
converted to a condo during the bubble
before the bubble that just burst, leaving us,
like a patch of floating garbage, slightly underwater
on a mortgage we secured with almost nothing down.

The highway, too, is an artery to the city's moldering heart,
but anatomy this isn't. The city sucks up
the oxygen we carry and, when done, ejects us
in the glare of a setting sun's sixty-story mirror.

Depleted, we stare dead ahead,
sway with the bus's every lurch.
Though I hold out hope of engaging your gaze,
of looking at and through you and having you
look at and through me, to find there
a different station, the state of play prevails:
power is hardwired. Frequent, random surges
move, heat, and light a world where
our view is ordained. If you see
something, say something.

My father was right: act as if someone is watching.
The intent was humane—
it would matter less that we're watched
than that we think we are. But in the gloaming,
when lights come on in the offices one by one,
the haphazard pattern on the blue building
looks like a punch card's.

We work later and later for less and less,
razor thin margin, razor thin tower
standing sentry over the city that encircles it.
Any day, I'm busting out.

Want in?

SL5 - INTERVALS

They're not renovating the Ferdinand so much as
gutting it for its skin, the Dudley Square landmark's
masonry tanned and tailored for another building's coat.
When the youngest of three boys, everything you own—
clothes, toys—is hand-me-down. We had the same
stuffed bear—first Luke, then Matt, then me.
By the time I arrived, Garfunkel had one eye,
stuffing protruding from the other socket
like an exposed optic nerve. He fared better than
his twin, though, Simon long since lost to the ravages
of time and toddlers who pull and tear. Funny to think
my parents named our crib companions for a folk-rock duo,
since music can, in some hands, signal rebellion: spirituals,
blues, soul and gospel, what Skippy White's sold
at Mass Ave and Washington. Although my parents were
well aware of what was erupting around them—
my father taught at a school in a redlined neighborhood
beset by rioters the day after Dr. King was shot—
there's a family photo (blue jackets, plaid pants,
bowl cuts for the boys) taken when I was six, hanging
in the house where I grew up. We're standing
in the back yard: lawn mown, azaleas in bloom,
a world from the South End's trash-strewn lots.
Next to it, individual shots: Luke in military dress,
Matt coat and tie, me white tux for prom.
We have the same hair, eyes, and cheekbones.

They tried rebranding Dover Street East Berkeley,
as if it would smell sweeter by another name,
but it wasn't until the elevated train came down that
galleries and restaurants moved in around the projects,
pushing out the pimps, hookers, and johns.
Rapid transit bus replaced the el, following the route
the tracks ran, but the city's drivers don't care.
They ignore dedicated lanes, drive in them anyway,
the buses forced to crawl at rush hour's pace.

So, yes, they may be renovating the Ferdinand,
gutting it for its skin, but the intervals between—
two years from boy to boy, three miles from what
we know to what we don't, from where my father
taught to where he raised us, from Downtown to
Dudley Square—seem as wide as they've ever been.

35 - DARK ARTS

It was the route to the mall by the McDonald's
where Bobby, first in our little gang to work,
got caught copping us food,
but memories are like buses: they run on loops.
Now I can't remember if Bobby's mother
talked the red-visored manager out of pressing charges.

I've wandered down so many sidetracks—
life's demos, bootlegs, and B-sides,
singles degraded by repeated play,
tape worn to grain my uncle wouldn't touch,
to grain that'll make you lose the line of your cut—
that way bled into way and there's no going back.

As a child I was obsessed with reboots,
perfection's pursuit, start mornings intent on it,
spy portent in a calendar—day of the week, week
of the month, month of the year—
walk with a measured gait to avoid
the sidewalk's cracks, and write on
paper as fresh as a field of snow,
in the painstaking cursive nuns taught,
grammatically perfect sentences
expressing stunted thoughts.

But no matter how careful, once you dive in—
winter coat, heavy boots—
angels pock the powder like Vitruvian men,
leave blemishes on pale, delicate skin.
In time, sunspots and wrinkles.
I should do something about them,
but life's elixir doesn't exist.
Science is replication. Alchemy's not.

37 - GUARDIAN ANGEL

A half moon that looks like
God licked his thumb and rubbed the sky
reminds me of half-moons my mother'd buy
at Hanley's bakery: frosting just right,
none too sweet, though being a brat
I refused to eat chocolate,
would cut them in half
and take only the vanilla parts.

A block up was Steve Slyne's,
whose crusty, eponymous owner would,
when my friends and I were old enough
to ride the bus the mile to the center,
yell at us if we took too long
deciding what we wanted from the candy rack.

Farther up was the bowling alley,
its crowded video game arcade
the middle school hangout, and all of it
north of Billings Field, where as teens
we'd go at night to drink.

Sometimes the cops would chase us,
but sometimes they wouldn't
and no one was ever arrested and no one
ever got hurt until, that is,
Brian drove home drunk
and Dave, in the passenger seat
when he blew through a stop sign,
wore for a year a metal halo.

Home Front

When I was eight, the route ended
at the veterans' hospital where
the medevacs came and went
and I volunteered to bring patients
from their rooms to hear mass
in the chapel near the entrance.

The hospital's chaplain, you see,
never delivered a sermon,
whereas up at St. T's
I'd be stuck listening
to the parish priest explain
in painstaking detail
the relevancy to my daily life
of the week's gospel reading.

Bored, we'd sneak out after communion,
hit Anna's for a honey dip donut,
before they changed the recipe
to try and compete
with the Dunkie's that moved in
down the end of our street.

Absent a sermon, the chaplain's service
was sufficiently brief. We waited until
the dismissal, after which we played football
in the field behind the hospital, my brothers and I
and guys from the block, the Walshes and Spillanes,
whose youngest, Chris, would for a long time
remain my best friend, and once,
in a corner of the field, we built a cardboard fort
on a dirt mound the hospital dug up
to lay down a parking lot.

We were too young to know that
as we fought each other for control
helicopters we stopped
to watch land and take off
carried real soldiers
wounded in real wars.

Pets

There was the goldfish I managed to kill overfeeding it:
morning, after school, and again before bed;
and the gypsy moth caterpillar a well-struck extra-point
knocked from the Cool Whip container
I appropriated for its cage, which,
because my mother forbade me from keeping it
in the house, I kept on the porch,
regrettably the goal post when,
after they paved the field behind the hospital,
we played football in the back yard instead;
and I guess the stray dog Chris and I fed
the summer day we found it sniffing grease stains
by the dumpsters behind the pizza shop
across from the Dunkin' Donuts at the end of the block.

Still, the closest we ever really came to
having a pet were nights dad cooked lobster.
As the water boiled, he took them from the bag
and let them crawl around the kitchen floor.
We gave them exotic names, like Ivan and Igor,
and, betting nickels and dimes, raced them.
He joked that if we listened
we could, as he dropped them in the scalding water,
hear the lobsters scream, but I never did,
even as they sank and their hard, black shells
turned a tender red.

American Foursquare

That's what we lived in, as did Mrs. Gay
and Mrs. White beside her. Also,
the Dawsons, Fitzgeralds, DiRenzos, and Spillanes,
whose front porch was home base
for street-long games of Relievio,
the trick to winning which was to hop
backyard fences, use the garages as cover.
Be careful, though. The Fitzgeralds' fence is high
and, when wet, the top slat slippery. I should know:
I once bit through my tongue when I hit my chin on a picket.

Lining the street, offering summer shade,
were great oaks, remnants of a different epoch.
Hurricane Gloria felled one,
the rest razed by human means,
carved initials killing bark, then tree.
What remained was so barren, asphalt and concrete.

Mrs. Gay died and though I heard the Dawsons divorced,
a Spillane still guards home base,
Chris's brother Mark with two girls,
like no-longer-so-little Mikey DiRenzo,
whose parents' yard, before being subdivided,
was the scene of more than one imaginary war,
the house built on the carved-out lot
twice since bought and sold.

When Mrs. White passed, new owners
gutted the interior, replaced the vinyl siding,
assembled a prefab basket in the driveway
so the kids can play two-on-two like we did.
The city planted fresh saplings too,
and though the young trees don't yet offer
the shade their forebears did, given time
they'll grow, tender acorns as weapons
for the next generation of mock warriors to throw.

Cicadas

Years condensed to a season seems
existence to pity, but who doesn't squeeze life
into narrow measures of time we deem
free—a weekend or week? Maybe two. Rife

is the routine that rules our periodic
worlds. 8am and already 90 degrees, my shirt
dark blue where I've sweated through the fabric.
The bus driver, when I board, is curt.

AC feels nice, but other riders, who
won't take their bags off empty seats,
stare straight ahead. What would they do
if I sat down anyway, dripping in the heat?

Would—from the friction or frustration,
backs drenched—anger flare?
When we finally pull in, the station
is so crowded I don't care

if I jolt other commuters. We're pinballs,
really. Skip the escalator unless a train arrives
on the lower platform and like an inverted waterfall
disembarking passengers pour up the stairs. A wife-

beater's never a good idea. Though,
to be honest, neither were pegged jeans
and the collars, at thirteen, we turned in on Polo
shirts. We split summer mornings between

Mike's and Chris's, played basketball
in the Spillanes' narrow driveway, ping-pong
in the DiRenzos' basement. Afternoons, we'd haul
it on our bikes to the river, long

before the feds mandated the state clean
it, before they put up the Home Depot where
the abandoned drive-in screen
stood and extended the route there.

Throwing beer bottles older teens drank at night
into the river to watch them sink, we tried to keep
cool in the shade, never considered the blight,
as I don't the moisture that seeps

down the cheap, concrete walls and stains
them and the platform on which I and, if you must,
the guy in the wife-beater, wait to take the next train.
I see it every day; my disgust,

through exposure, long since killed.
Collateral damage: immersion,
mastery of frivolous skills—
behind-the-back dribble or serve with spin,

the log roll on the video game we played when tired
of basketball and ping-pong. Emerging at State Street,
collars and adolescent memories wilt in the heat.
I barely recognize the pursuit they inspired.

9 – Mirror Neurons

The dentist asked if I had
an eating disorder,
but it was a bad
habit of making hangovers shorter

by throwing up. Gastric acid
corroded the enamel,
and nicotine—from a flaccid
cigarette, soft packs of Camels,

lit to mask the taste of puke in my mouth—
stained. Of the nights I vomited
there were too many to count,
and there was the time I plummeted

from a fourth floor fire escape
and managed, somehow, to bypass death,
walk away with but a few scrapes
and bruises. The provincial mindset

dies hard; symbols are signifiers,
they point to things that may
not be there but acquire
the power of totems anyway:

cable knit sweaters, Scally caps,
fresh pints of Guinness,
which, if bars don't clean their taps,
taste like really thick piss.

Still, I'd have slurped piss porridge,
brought bowl to mouth to achieve a state
in which I could find the courage
to ask a girl out on a date.

Even when Stephanie
slipped into my room wearing
nothing but the sheerest lingerie
I somehow ended up no nearer

to sex. That summer a group of us—
Jason, Adam, Greg, and Ben—
lived a mile from campus.
Stephanie was, at 21, broken.

I was merely lost,
sitting on the porch in twilight
drinking what I thought
I should—Jameson's—every night.

Symbol and thought reverberated
like loud voices caught between
narrow canyon walls, like conjugated
images whose reflections can be seen

in opposing mirrors and reflections
of those mirrors and the whole circuit
of infinite reflections
that recede into the polished surfaces.

Years later, from a friend's walk-up,
we'd watch the St. Patrick's Day parade,
then move a block up
to the Beer Garden, where I stayed

until last call, lace curtain diaspora
trying to be working-class
trying to be Irish, beer flowing faster
and faster as the night passed.

Once, during a fight, like flak
the bottles flew and so that became
the headline that became a paperback
that was adapted into a screenplay

for an Oscar-winning movie,
the film version of whose stage musical
will be issued in a Collector's Edition DVD
that includes, among the other special

features, a making-of documentary.
God forbid it's sold in just
a plain old box. We'd barely
recognize it, barely recognize us.

17 - Worship

From the balcony of the third floor
in one of a row of perfectly average triple-deckers
along the route from Andrew to Everett Square,
there was over the stately, wood-shingled
historical society and its volunteer-kept lawn
an unimpeded view:
used car lots, tarred rooftops, rusting fence, a dead oak,
the glass-littered street where the car was stolen
and the street, a block over, where it turned up stripped,
all of it interrogation-lit seared summer evenings
by the glare off the Hancock Tower,
whose oversized panels, like mirrors,
caught on its western face the colors of sunset,
time running, as it hasn't since, backwards,
image of a progressively yellow, orange and red orb,
pulling behind it pink, purple, and bruised black night,
sliding up a monument raised in vain to silent gods,
themselves but the reflected images
to which we've always prayed.

65 - ALLSTON

When I moved, I begged friends,
traded beer for muscle.
At a certain age, though, you really should hire movers.
You've got a job; spend the money.
The friends? They're scattered anyway:
other states, other cities, the exurbs of this one.

Dangling from a tent a light rain
drummed with dumb fingers,
Chinese lanterns danced in the wind.
The guests mingling on the country club's patio
shivered. I haven't seen Raj since,
job, house, and kids a shifting fault.
Sure, you can tell time by strata,
but that doesn't mean across the canyon
geologists won't find the rock's match
thirty feet up the opposite wall.

There was no AC in the apartment we shared.
Summers, temperature near 90,
barely a breeze penetrating threadbare curtains,
I slept on the deck,
bedroll thin cartilage between me
and the beer-stained two-by-fours.
Through the rail's slats, I could see
the moon rise over the house next door,
half-shell Mary luminescent in the front yard.

There comes a moment in every life
when being alone stops being exhilarating,
but you're too old for a roommate.
So I looked at studios,
all I could afford without a second income.

Unbuttoned overcoat open
to autumn's unforecasted warmth,
purple scarf a priest's stole around my neck,
I would, to try and slow my descent,
grab the dangling ends like a rip cord.
At night through curtains that, when parted,
lay bare the beating heart behind the brick exterior
of the apartment next door,
forms floated in the lamplight as the neighbors
put their young son to bed.

To watch the intimate routines
of those I no more than greeted
was wrong. Yes, they were
the silhouettes of routines
and not the quotidian articles themselves,
but light and shadow have nuance and there is,
in diverse shades, essence.

To stare at a stranger is to stare at the sun.
The glare is why we look away.

18 - A Dorchester Eclogue

Pantry Pizza was Patty's Pantry, The Banshee Vaughn's
and though I'd catch the stench of dirty dish water
from the door to the kitchen around the side,
I loved Venice's chicken and broccoli pasta.
That is until the night you ran into Bruce
investigating a murder whose victim had
dragged himself inside. Yellow tape
marks a line you shouldn't cross.

The Boys and Girls Club where I worked
is buried a block off the avenue behind the laundromat
where, while I waited for my clothes to dry,
shopping-cart moguls hawked bootleg DVDs.
Like something on late night TV, before cable,
the audio on the one you bought ran
a half second behind the video. Only thing missing:
the national anthem at the end of the credits.

On the billboard atop its shuttered building
there's the outline of an advertisement for
West Coast Video. *Yes, landmarks change*
and Irish bars are now Vietnamese restaurants.
I never tried pho, brought peanut butter and jelly
for lunch every day from first to twelfth grade
and had a mother who never cooked anything
more exotic than lasagna. To her, salt was a spice,
water a marinade, and though I've been told her
mushroom rolls are addictive, I don't, as a rule, eat fungus.
Try something new; you're not a kid anymore.

From storefront churches preachers thunder
at congregants perched on metal chairs.
The faithful stare at me standing in the doorway.
So what if this single room of worship doesn't
remind you of the parish where you went to mass?
You don't get to determine what's holy.
What will you do? Slash tires? Key cars?
Occupy parking spaces with patio furniture?

4 - Sightlines

The route's the same—along Atlantic from South Station
to North—but the elevated highway that
cut through you like a gangrenous wound is gone,
so too the traces of almost twenty years of construction
it took to pull the rusting hulk underground.
I could drive your surface roads blind,
but my mind's map is dated. There are new lights,
new on-ramps, new off-ramps, new lanes for new turns.

First dates were dinners in the North End,
late-night walks along the harbor, but there are
new hotels, new offices, new shadows cast on a park
that's sprouted where the highway used to be.
Views are coveted, perspective craved,
what water grants us: open vistas, arched skies,
a glimpse of horizon, a hint of other islands.

On bright Saturday afternoons, the line for the Aquarium
stretches to the avenue. I could walk like a penguin,
my nose too crawling like a snail on the glass
of the great tank around which the long ramp winds.
Of course, water bends light. I can snap a pencil in half
by dropping it in a glass, and the fronds of sea grass
that swayed in imperceptible currents at the bottom of the tank
weren't where I believed them to be.

But that's true universally, which means
I can measure the distance between us by the parallax,
the difference in your position along two lines of sight,
say my right and left eyes as, staring at you
out a window a kid scratched his initials in,
I close first one and then the other. The difference grows
the closer we get. So while I admire the Escher-like way
your skyline ascends from cornices crowning
nineteenth-century buildings to antennas
atop twenty-first-century towers, you aren't
where I want you to be. I can reach out
and touch you, bump my nose on your glass.

I'm swimming in circles; you're a twenty-gallon tank.

57 - THOUGHT EXPERIMENT

The Last Drop always lived up to its name,
serving until the latest possible legal moment.
The bartender went to grammar school with me.
Even as the place emptied, he would slip
us one more. Those nights, our routine was the same:
take-out from Dragon Chef back at the apartment
where I'd pass out on the couch with a movie
in the VCR and tobacco in my lower lip,

the brown expectoration oozing down my chin
to stain the front of my shirt. I never caught
more than the first 20 minutes of *Goodfellas*.
It wasn't even my crib. Jay, Eric, and Brian rented it.
When one of them moved out to get married, Austin
moved in. Brian was the first of us to tie the knot,
the first to say he wanted what they tell us
we're supposed to want. I'm sure he meant it.

I haven't seen him in, oh, I don't know,
five years, and I have to admit his girlfriend was
lovely. We've all since married, split, married again,
and, yet, the odd times we get together, seem unchanged,
which could be due to the unlikely scenario
that our selves were fully formed at twenty-one, or because,
like objects dropped from a moving train,
we change at a pace that remains unchanged

until we hit the ground. Inertia is a property,
not a force. From where we stand in the open door
of the boxcar, what we discard appears to fall
in a straight line; from the vantage of a field
through which the tracks cut, its trajectory
is a curve. It moves simultaneously forward
and down. We meant to organize a pub crawl,
a reunion of sorts, but invariably failed

to get around to planning it. There are, of course,
the usual excuses, the mundane tasks, normal
obligations: lunches to pack, dinners to cook,
memos to draft. What would we do in their absence,
set in motion by forces beyond our control, forces
that hover forever at the edge of our peripheral
vision? They disappear when we turn to look,
exist, in fact, beyond our inertial frame of reference.

43 - Nucleus Accumbens

The State House's gold dome crowns the low hill
the bus scales as it skirts the Common,
city spied through turning trees on the other side.
Barren paths crisscross the pale grass.

The driver leans on the horn at cars parked at the stop
before the monument to the 54th Massachusetts Regiment.
Cars coming in the other direction idle, respond in kind,
blare at the unseen source of congestion down Beacon Street.

It's clear we're in a rush.

Winter's first storm looms. It starts as rain,
streams like sperm down the bus's steam-filled windows.
September's weather flouts the equinox,
but October, skeins of geese flying
migratory routes in late afternoon's dark sky,
swings between what was and will be, warmth and gloom.

Ancients tracked seasons by moon, stars,
the patterns of the prey they hunted.
They built monuments to measure in the light's angle
the time to plant. Memorial and Labor Days
are arbitrary bookends only between which
was white once fashionably acceptable.

When we go home, the tide leaves on empty beaches
unbroken lines of seaweed. We sat on the deck's
rail doing the crossword, sat shoulder to shoulder,
skin to skin, growing colder and colder.
Glowing like a cigarette, the sun slipped behind
the trees on the other bank of the inlet.

How long ago it seems. Still we rush.

The rare among us have a third eye
to perceive the concentric rings of the pond
from which we crawl out on shore.

Fourteen years from plaster cast to bronze relief:
black soldiers and white officer. Daily we pass it
without a glance, dodge tourists trying
to appreciate beauty and sacrifice between the SUVs,
our reptilian brains flashing *more, more.*

111 - Emerald Cities

The gangrenous, double-decked, cantilevered bridge
whose twin highway came down almost a decade ago
rises from a tunnel by the monument of the battle
where they aimed for the whites of their eyes.
The rusting green metal infects the majesty
of everything it touches: stately brownstones
in the monument's gentrified square,
the river it spans, the dilapidated piers where it lands,
our memory of an American dream.

Four years I taught children whose families
arrived in a square mile of writhing humanity
as seemingly far from the gleaming city across the water
as what they'd left behind. From the commuter rail overpass,
they can see steel and glass. For every point on a map
how many lie beyond, climbing with the terrain
from knoll to mountain?

This city that shall be as on a hill: will new colonists
gain election, the trappings that are its outward sign?
They'll spend their lives at two jobs,
scratching in the yards of vinyl-sided homes
bought with what they saved by depriving themselves
of pleasure in the time that's left. The ancient blessing
was more life, passed from generation to generation.
And what's wrong with that, to labor for children
who will labor for theirs, who will labor for theirs?

The bus I took to teach runs up Washington.
Across Route 16 it turns, turns again, parallels the highway.
At odd stops, passengers hop on and off,
the terminus Woodlawn—mausoleum, columbarium,
acres of grass home to the tombs, urns, and coffins
of strangers and loved ones and strangers' loved ones.

The cemetery, green, well tended, is open to the public.

39 - COMMUNION

In the rush of disembarking commuters
a pigeon ascends to a pipe across the span
of the arch at the station's back entrance
from the walk where moments before
it'd pecked at the crumbs discarded by those
who are, to some, no more than the careless.

But what can they know of hunger or the indignity
of eating breakfast in public a speck at a time?
Know of begging from those who've never
known hunger or the indignity of eating
breakfast in public a speck at a time?
Of reading in a restaurant's glass front a menu
from which they can but dream of ordering?

The famine's victims were sometimes found
at the roadside with green, syllogistic mouths:
if I eat the cow and the cow eats the grass,
I, too, can chew blades. Little did they know
transubstantiation isn't literal.

16 – GENEALOGY

The $300-a-month apartment I shared with two
friends after college was infested; we
golfed with the mice we caught in the glue
traps. Though I was separated from my family

by only six miles, we didn't speak. My mother, she
knew well how to want and wanted so much
she'd want for you. Shadows of bare trees
thrown by a low sun streak the sludge-

covered snow that pocks the route
my father took to teach. Out the bus's plastic
windows, behind Burger King and a church's blue
spire, you can still see the red brick.

After wrestling a kid for his gun, he retired.
Before he died, my wife stopped talking to or about
her father, called him little better than a liar.
The Sunday we split pitchers at Applebee's out

shopping in the plaza along the highway near
the abandoned Bickford's, she read
while I watched the Giants—his team, she said.
Shoes stuck to the floor, reek of stale beer.

55 - The Right Light

Boylston Street, up which the bus runs, intersects
Mass Ave. Where it crosses the Pike, we stood one night
in pouring rain too stubborn to resolve the fight
we'd had about something I can't now recollect.

We fought a lot back then, our new love's bloom fading,
our first winter as a couple falling, too soon to tell
if what we thought we had would be perennial,
if what we admired in the other's soft shading

would be lost stepping out from under the studio's
tungsten umbrellas. Daily life can be so bright;
poetry can't always hold up in the harsh light.
I stop at the library, return the Rimbaud

collection I checked out three years ago. The fee:
$30. The summer we spent together
I bought her a small gift, an old novel, leather-
bound, title embossed. We were in England. Ivy

crept up the walls of a terrace and bees hovered,
lured by the garnish in glasses on tables at
the Trout, the stone pub where, late afternoons, we sat
under umbrellas, read, drank, and so fell in love.

As we walked the path back to town, the grass in glades
on either side looked divided, half a halo
above half rooted in the earth, and in the glow
of the lambent summer air, gnats skipping from blade

to blade were, at that magic hour, lit so softly
their silhouettes were almost the size of brass door
knobs and I could make out individual spores
of pollen on the breezes holding them aloft.

But we came home, got jobs, bought a third-floor condo,
the strange people in the pictures in the triptych
on the hallway bookshelf gone. And so we make lists:
of things we'll do and, oh, the places we will go.

Still it is to work that I walk back and forth, far
from the restaurants lining this elegant street,
past the warehouse that collapsed in nine-alarm heat,
the waste transfer station, and the lot where Moe parks.

He's right: eat well, stay fit, die anyway. His ribs,
though they're truck-cooked, are easily the best around.
With all the petty proscriptions by which we're bound,
it just feels so fucking good to strap on a bib.

Even here, on the rim of this city canyon,
the thin films—oil-slicked puddles—left on clean windows
by washer's squeegees, collect in tiny rainbows
the weak light of a bitter winter's distant sun.

52:71 - STAGE FRIGHT

Circles of light cast by street lamps form
Venn diagrams. My silhouettes emerge
in the intersections as the ones before them
thin like cheap wine tipped toward the glass's rim.
You can't show me anything different from
the shadow striding behind me in the light
of a lamp I haven't reached, or the shadow
rising to meet me in the light of the lamp
I already passed. You can only measure
the angle from the vertex which is that
place and time here and now: me.

It took two buses to reach it. The 52 stopped
at the end of the block, ran all the way
to Watertown, where I switched to the 71.
I was, even after graduating, still working
the front desk at the college gym, hesitating
on the threshold of a door held open
by an overly solicitous concierge waiting
for me to slip a crisply folded twenty
into the breast pocket of his crimson,
white-piped, brass-buttoned jacket.

I was afraid to enter, to assume the role
everyone had, in their minds, written for me,
to don, like the doorman, my costume—
power tie, scarf, overcoat. I missed my cue
and now, in the third act, I spend my time
shuffling on and off, a bit player in a massive,
nine-hour production with an unsurprisingly
limited run. I recite my lines with desperate,
cringe-worthy brio, rattling the seats
in the small theater's back row, where I can
make out my parents in the sparse audience.

They know there are limits, have known
much longer than I have my precise ones.
Tired, they'll sneak out at intermission
for a bite at the Chili's that used to be across
from the entrance to the tunnel for buses
pulling in and out of Harvard Station.
For my wife, I'll go on, linger upstage
walking dark streets, measuring angles
of shadows thrown by street lamps
like floodlights on the curtains drawn tight
against fast approaching night.

89 - HE WAS MY AGE WHEN HE FIRST PAINTED A PINK LADY

Willem de Kooning used what material he could—
paper, canvas, cardboard—to make art.

Fine cracks would appear in the oil, which he'd
apply and scrape off, apply and scrape off,
the layers collecting like sediment, the paint
spreading like a desert wash. With newspapers,
he'd mop up the excess and the inverted print
of a column or ad turned his images to text,
lets us know now what they bought then.
When done, he'd start over, trace the image's outline
on fresh canvas, apply new paint, scrape it off,
apply more, disfigured women growing only
more disfigured through the course of his career,
much as we grow only more disfigured
through the course of ours, no matter the mornings
I'm ashamed to admit I moisturize in the vain hope
no one will notice wrinkles radiating from the corners
of my eyes, no matter the mornings I'm ashamed
to admit what I was like before the onset of
wrinkles radiating from the corners of my eyes.

Coming up Broadway, the bus crests Winter Hill.
Behind it, sprouting like great oaks from thickets
of triple-deckers, there's Bunker Hill Monument,
Schrafft's factory, Hood's smokestack, that awful
green bridge, and newer plants belching fumes
that on a day like this dissolve like breath.
Bodegas line the strip along which Irish mobs
waged war. I played basketball at Trum Field,
got coffee at the Lebanese place, and Gewurztraminer
at the new wine store to impress the girls I met.
Slowly, canvas over canvas, the pink lady
begat pink ladies: Lainy, Jess, Adina, two Kims.
Yet, despite the layers I apply and scrape off,
the images I transpose leave traces
of memories that make me wince.

Heidi spent the party dancing with someone else.
I spent it in the corner watching her.

83 - ARCHAEOPTERYX

Risotto was the caterer's specialty. I spent hours
in his kitchen on Beacon Street rinsing it from china
and scrubbing it from the pots it simmered in.

Some days, I can still smell it on my hands,
along with the slightest breath of cold prime rib
and slightly sickening bouquet of gray, day-old salmon.

As bright and beautiful as they are,
cardinals nesting in an eave of a porch
carry on their talons the worm's scent,

just as lions do the stench of the carcasses
they rip apart on the veldt, where last week
scientists found a nine-year-old's two-million-year-old skull.

It's been years since I bussed tables and washed dishes.
You would have thought the smells would dissipate, but
who can, despite the lengths he will go to,
conceal the less refined aspects of his evolution?
To wit: breaking my trumpet in seventh grade
carrying it to school in the bottom of my book bag
because I was afraid what the other kids might think,
and for years gleaning only an impression
of the world through which I passed because
I refused to wear glasses whose lenses were too thick.

I faked injuries for attention, threatened suicide
on a pier in Rhode Island after drinking too much vodka,
tried after too much wine to claim the mild abrasions
I'd suffered during a relatively antiseptic life
were an emotional match for Lainy's childhood
with a single mother who didn't quite speak the language.

I was once asked in an interview to pinpoint the moment
I became who I am, the person they wanted to hire,
as if life were stop-motion, as if we can reconcile
position and direction, but I'm never who I am,
only who I was and yet long to be.

My teeth and tail might be a reptile's
and the embarrassing fossils of my experience
preserved in layers of sediment,
but yet I hope the wings I'm sprouting lead to flight.

47 - TATTOOS

It doesn't make sense: the route cuts against
the city's grain. Though a paltry three miles
for the pigeons that defile the station,
it's an hour's crawl from Ruggles to Central Square.
Shafts of a setting sun's light perforating
an overcast sky evoke the heavens masters used
to decorate upper edges of canvases
in museums we pass near the Fens.

Ave Louis Pasteur seems like a detour.
I went to school there, rarely class,
was asked to leave in eighth grade. The next right
is the hospital—Beth Israel Deaconess—
where my girlfriend worked when I met my wife.

Six months from first date to the night I proposed,
another eight until the protracted bus trip
to the parlor where we had our wedding bands
engraved in ink on our left hands. Like everyone,
we fight—once over a bread knife, once
a glass of water. For that, we had an audience—

her college friend, Mike, playing George Segal
to our Liz and Dick. There was pain, always is,
needle on bone. We chose for a design a gift
I gave her: a silver ring of shallow waves,
one on top of the other, that crest, then ebb,
like parabolas I might explain with calculus.

Math is part of it, data to determine
where and when the buses run.
So many strive to be half of one,
the circle the symbol of marriage.
But rings come off, fingers grow fat, gold,
the alchemy of love and pain, is readily tarnished.
It's easy, is it not, to leave them in a drawer?

No, ink and needle afforded permanence,
permanent, at least, as we are.

51 - TESSERACT

There's a story my father tells about a driver
on the trolley line that quit running along
the last leg of the bus's route forty years ago.
Joe Kelly stopped one night between stops,
invited passengers to a party at the Clancys'—
who lived next to Mount St. Joseph's—and
had to leave a half-hour later at the clang of
the bell of the car stuck behind on the tracks.
There's what happened, my father's version
of what happened, my version of my father's
version, your interpretation of my version
and, should you retell it, your audience's
interpretation of your interpretation of my
version of my father's version of the story.

When Amy and I lost track of time, we were
lucky to catch the last train out of Park Street,
got to Cleveland Circle too late for a bus.
We had to call for a ride. Standing where
I stand now, looking at me standing where
I stood then, wondering what I was thinking
imagining what Amy's father, a man who
used silence, was thinking standing where he
stood eyeing his daughter and her laughably
thin date, trying to distinguish defiance
from a mistake, my present me wonders
if his present him remembers my memory.

Driving back and forth to college along
the route, trips accumulated, the car like
the neurons that inscribe pathways between
synapses. They create the means to remember:
the times of day, if the sun was out, if mist was
rising from the thawing reservoir, if I drove
with the window down, arm hanging in
the breeze flowing past my parents' beat-up
Honda, plastic Mary glued to the dashboard.

But then I can't hold it all in my head.
It's too big, like one of those paintings
in a museum or the apse of a church.
To examine any one part of it, to notice tiny
cracks in the paint, saints' elongated fingers,
is to ignore the top of the canvas where
otherworldly light breasts the heavens.
To remember any one stretch of route is
to climb the great pyramid of association—
the monument store, its model gravestones
littering the front lawn, and the caterer
where Bobby's mother got us jobs after
he was fired from McDonald's; we loaded
and unloaded trucks with serving pans
and boxes of boxed lunches too heavy
for weak arms. But to remember is to forget,
forget where the bus runs past the street
on which Amy grew up, the path where
I'd linger in hopes of pretending to
casually run into her because I was
too afraid to call and ask her out.

The bus is full. For each thought, an object:
me, the annoying couple talking
too loudly about their weekend plans,
the kid rapping under his breath to what's
playing through his headphones,
the old woman with her shopping basket
(bundled, like Mrs. Whatsit, beyond
human recognition), three young women
I would have once felt the need to impress
with studied indifference, the girl reading
a textbook, her mother on the next seat
variously reprimanding her brother, who
won't sit still, and watching a daughter
learning in a language she hasn't learned.

93 – FEAR OF FALLING

The collapsed right side of the face
of the man standing next to me at the stop
looks like someone punches it daily.
The bus we wait to take is one of two
my wife and I took to meet our financial advisor,
the year we needed one, which is to say,
the year we could afford it.

Each time, the message the same:
save for tomorrow, defer until tomorrow,
which is to say deprive yourself until tomorrow.
If you meet your goals, reward yourself
with dinner on the way home.
Eat at the bar. Split the appetizer, skip the dessert.

Ignore the guy with the half caved-in face
now begging for fare. He's a bad investment.
If he starts talking to himself, put headphones on.
You don't have to listen to music,
but having the buds in means you don't
have to pretend to listen to disembodied rants and,
by a miracle we'll call the distributive property of sense,
if you can pretend you can't hear him,
you can pretend you can't see him.

But much as we resist the gravitation of others,
we walk through the world as worlds, depressing
time and space like they're old mattresses. At night
we lay our heads on separate sides of the bed;
come morning we've rolled to the middle. There
you can hear your wife scream. If you're lucky,
she can hear you. I take the bus one way, walk back,
weather unseasonable. I sweat under the bulk of
a hooded sweatshirt I don as a sop to the kid I'm not.

I'm supposed to have gone farther than this, farther than
a city bus can take me. But what recourse? Steal a car?
Charlestown is the car theft capital of America,
so every movie set here tells us. God forbid
a two-bit hood use a gun instead of an equity fund.

28 - GOSPEL MUSIC

Walk far enough now, my left knee gets sore;
it's what buses are for, the roads they run on,
some planned—laid out in a grid—
some unplanned, worn by use, cobbled, then paved.
Farmers farm the farms they call home.
When they built factories, they built dorms to go with them.
Until horses drew trolleys, it never dawned on anyone
to live one place and work another.

The first farm needed no tending.
We named the livestock, but lacked restraint.
Funny how the mind fixates on what it can't know.
The Torah tells it well: how we fell.
We've wandered since—
across continents, across oceans, across the sky
in winged cylinders that glint in a setting sun's light.

Trickles become streams, streams rivers, rivers torrents.
Torrents flood cities, the floods collect in neighborhoods
like tidal pools as the surge recedes—
from Italy to the North End, from Poland to South Boston,
from the shtetl to Warren Street and Blue Hill Ave.

When waves roll in, sucking up the water in their paths,
they reveal, before they break, bare slopes of sand,
but even a tsunami must look from space
like a ripple on a pond's surface and,
though the spirit departs, there's flesh
to nourish the grass that grows on graves.

The minyans moved, their hulls remain.
Etched in stone, Stars of David adorn
the churches that were synagogues,
filled now by new waves of congregants, ceaseless,
ever rolling, ever washing up on these celestial shores
a person, a family, a village at a time.

On the 1200 block, the new Baptist church
overlooks the avenue. From it wafts
the choir's voices, keyboard's accompaniment.
Mechanics lounging in the garage's shade
listen to merengue that to unversed ears sounds
like a record spun too fast. Dressed in Sunday best,
old women bend like the accordion buses
that ply the route to Dudley Square.

They lean on canes, press pamphlets in palms
as people pass. Travel agents, they mouth
hymn and prayer. A few more weary days, they say.
Hallelujah, by and by, I'll fly away.

60 - 4ᵀᴴ GRADE ART

A house was a lop-sided box,
triangle on top, front door
a rectangle, windows squares
with half circles hung as valances.

From a roof shingled in trapezoids
protruded a chimney.
It exhaled loops of brown smoke
under a yellow sun whose rays
were like the lines that
mark on the face of a clock
the hours and the minutes.

Across the top of the page
flew quickly scribbled birds,
checks, really, drawn in black crayon
with flicks of the wrist and tonight,
waiting for the bus, watching
the silhouettes of two gulls disappear
in the twilight over the hospitals,

I realize, if nothing else
on those 8.5 by 11 inch canvases,
I got the birds right.

214:216 - CHAOS THEORY

When walking the dogs at night, stop to enjoy the stillness
of your little corner of a city that's never still:
sound of tires running over metal seams
between the concrete slabs of the highway overpass,
wind stirring the creepers twined about
the spikes of a wrought-iron fence. On the curbside,
pine needles and dead leaves mark where the snow banks,
now melted, were piled during winter by passing plows.
You can map moraines and model wind with fractals,
but how to know what to know before we know it?
From data, we hope new species of thought arise.
Like flies' eggs, fecundity guarantees propagation.
After all, predators lurk—ads, slogans, sound bites,
bullies who sense in everything and one different from them
an ineffable threat. For an idea to reach maturity, how many
must be sacrificed, subsumed by accumulated data,
the store of which swells like a thunderhead.

Rain starts to fall. Sheets of it sweep in over the bay.
Warmer and cooler currents form patterns
of lighter and darker water on its agitated surface.
On the sea wall, a circular picnic table lies on its side,
the umbrella's hole empty. Below it, the beach's dunes
are eroding, houses up the hill from the yacht club
threatened, the pine needles and leaves washed out,
thoughts lost in spats and the Blackberry's vibrations.
At dawn, I walk the dogs, put the coffee on.
On the bus, a kid brags to his friends about
beating the shit out of someone. The rain stops,
the sun emerges. The new high school gleams
in the wet light. Beside it, the old one looms.
How proud were the men who built it.

15 – I will die in Boston on a Saturday afternoon

riding the bus home from Haymarket,
my backpack full of produce bought at remainder,
the same produce sold at supermarkets, about to turn,
bruises and brown spots already spoiling
the peaches' soft skin.

The bus will be late. I'll pass the time,
call my parents, text my wife,
but I'll not mention this keenest of premonitions.
I hope they don't hold it against me,
the knowledge I don't share,

knowledge a thing universally resented because Adam and Eve
stole Yahweh's hoard of it and the punishment
was what Zeus meted out to Sisyphus,
who thought he was as smart as a god.
Then its form was apple, a symbol universally recognized.
I will have bought four for a dollar.
They will rest in my backpack at the base of my spine.

When, at last, the bus pulls up,
I'll board, breath shallow and labored,
as I've noticed it growing shallow and labored
on my walk to and from work.
When the attack comes, the ambulance
will be slow to arrive because traffic behind the bus,
which pulled only part of the way over, was stuck.

Last night, two riders attacked the driver;
he wouldn't let them smoke.
I smoked, still do sometimes. Don't regret it,
won't regret it sitting there, slumped in a cupped blue seat,
heart overheating. I'll remember the decks, porches,
bars, cars, and dinner tables where I lit up,
the skies I admired as a single round ember
flared and faded with every drag,
the strangers I eyed in neon barlight,
the landscapes that whipped by at 75 miles per hour,
the wind that took the ash,
the philosophy, the literature, the history
we thrashed out between us.

SL1 - Dun Aengus

Beyond curvilinear walls, a gray ocean beckons:
a photograph in a pack I snapped that summer
of jagged coastline and green fields.
What compelled the Celts across Europe
to a 300-foot high cliff on one of
the continent's last outcrops? There were far more
inviting places to stop along the way. Was it fear,
dawning consciousness of greener grass elsewhere?

From such a height—no wall fully enclosing
the spare tabletop of land the semicircles
leave exposed to the sheer drop—all is void.
Walls breached, arms outstretched, flight
would have been the last resort. Under a new moon,
the plane took off, hauling me on tourism's well-oiled
conveyor belt to Ireland and back, to Aran and back,
in a jitney across the island to the prehistoric
fort and back. I remember the family vacations
to visit my grandmother, aunts, uncles, and cousins,
and the Rube Goldberg machine at the terminal, where
as a kid, I was transfixed by the closed circuit
of lifts and roller-coaster-like tracks bringing
the balls back to the same place each time.

This was before they dug the third harbor tunnel,
and the bus ran its route under the seaport
through the landfill used to build up the flats
that once stretched into the harbor at low tide.
The airport itself sits where mud was once laid bare
twice daily by the moon's gravitational pull.
Here, we've temporarily tamed nature; there,
elemental forces prevail. In a quayside pub,
I learned to produce a shiny, hand-cut Celtic cross
with the lining in a pack of Silk Cut: a few folds,
here and there a half-moon tear in the silver paper.
The receding tide left behind it a reeking beach.
On black water, the silhouettes of fishing trawlers
bobbed as they have since they were hide-fit curraghs.

My mother left Ireland not long after John Glenn
orbited Earth, boarding a plane, not as tourist
but pilgrim, and I can't decide what takes more
courage, that or riding a Roman candle into space.
I hope that with her impulsiveness and temper
I inherited the same sense of the possible,
for even then I suspected shadows would intrude,
sweeping, as the sun descended, over dark faces
of offices staring back across a downtown street,
gibbous moon rising, marbled by black veins
of antennae protruding from a forty-story roof.

I see the Celts now, huddled at the cliff's edge
I captured at 400 speed in the dim light of a damp day.
They're braced against the ocean gale, holding back
long, plaited hair. Some want to believe they
worshiped storms there, but I picture them lowering
boats into rough surf to map the currents they hoped
would take them over the horizon. Maybe for kicks
they placed in each a message etched in dry seaweed,
a lamb or pig they trained to tack against the wind,
like that Russian dog or the silver-suited monkeys
NASA strapped in test rockets, about the time
my mother fixed her gaze on this distant shore.

1 - VOYAGERS TO THE WEST

My mother came from a windswept farm,
cows and sheep, a three-room house. I remember
the trips there, cream on the milk. Like her,
aroused by better prospects, others came,
in the thousands, tens of thousands.
Though Boston's streets were cow paths and
the bus routes seem as random, there must be
some intent—who gets where, who wins out.

What does the straight shot up Mass Ave
from Dudley Square to Harvard through the Back Bay
tell us? It runs north-northwest, like a trip, say,
from the Gaza Strip to Paris by way of
Monaco's lush hills, a short skip from the fading
Revivalist station that hasn't seen a trolley or a train
since they razed the elevated Orange Line
to the white cupolas crowning the college's domain.

I drank at The Boathouse, Sports Grille,
Bow and Arrow, when done, ate late night at
The Tasty, all gone, rent control abolished.
What I didn't do: attend class or study.
Now at the route's opposite end, in sight
of the medical center where ambulances
rush victims of the city's violence, where kids
make headlines only for the shots they fire,
I work, worry about the mortgage, and occasionally
admire a pink sky—disappointment, I'm sure,
to forebears who scratched a meager life from

a granite outcrop in a callous ocean.
They'd have expected more;
I know my mother did. For months, we didn't talk
because I earned less at my first job than
what Harvard's tuition cost, wasted four years and
what my father got when his mother died
to amount to this. So she thought.

Winter settles in, storm follows storm,
snow piles up. Young mothers push strollers
through the slush. City and transit
authorities fight over whose job it is
to keep the stops clear; the bus stops
in the street, traffic stuck, snarled for blocks.

201 - Imram

Age seventy, St. Brendan embarked with
a crew in little more than a hollow cork
to search for the Isles of the Blest,
where grain grew without work.

They found islands with birds that crew
in Latin and knew their vespers, with sheep
that grew bigger than oxen and waterfalls
that slid over cliffs straight into the deep.

They dodged towers of floating ice, tall as
mountains, hard and smooth as marble, but they
never found what they were looking for.
They reached these shores, some say,

because sailors claimed the light ofttimes flashed
green on the horizon when the sun set.
They who do business in great waters
like to tell tales, most of them tall you can bet,

but life being what it is
who among us would deprive their brethren
of stories of solace to distract them,
for just a moment, until when

balm is applied. Patron saint of sailors,
Brendan became; a church in his name
stands on the 201's inbound route,
on a median-divided street that, inflamed

by a late summer sun, pocked by chain stores,
could be any waterside commercial strip.
The air this clear, the tang of the river mouth's
marshes on the tongue, this morning I slipped

my desk's mooring in the back dormer of
the Victorian on the hill where,
most days, I just sit and watch the sky change—
from blue to pink to gloaming—hoping there's

time still to push my shallow-bottomed boat
out into the currents to explore,
to range the coast and map its contours,
marking the shoals and reefs lying offshore.

And though I promised others I'd not lose
sight of land, go where I shouldn't go,
the horizon beckons. I want to see
what I can't see, know what I don't know.

Notes on the Text

SL5 – Intervals

blues, soul and gospel, what Skippy White's sold
at Mass Ave and Washington

Skippy White's is now located on Columbus Avenue in Egleston Square.

36 – Panels, Cicadas

the log roll on the video game we played when tired

For those readers who must know, the video game was the Commodore 64 version of World Games.

65 – Allston

Allston is a neighborhood in Boston known for being home to a large number of college students and recent graduates.

18 – A Dorchester Eclogue

What will you do? Slash tires? Key cars?
Occupy parking spaces with patio furniture?

Using furniture and other objects to save on-street parking spaces one has shoveled after a snowstorm is a time-honored Boston tradition, recently codified as a city-sanctioned regulation that allows residents to use space savers up to forty-eight hours after a storm. Of course, many car owners leave their space savers out for much longer than that, thereby greatly aggravating their neighbors. Not that I, personally, have ever been aggravated by the practice. Never.

4 – Sightlines

so too the traces of almost twenty years of construction
it took to pull the rusting hulk underground.

The Big Dig, which tore down the old Route 93 Expressway and replaced it with a highway that runs under the city, officially began construction in 1991 and ended in 2007, when the partnership between the Massachusetts Turnpike Authority, the state agency that oversaw the project, and the private contractor that served as the project manager was dissolved. To date, it remains the most expensive single highway construction project in American history.

stretches to the avenue. I could walk like a penguin,

A line from a cheesy commercial for the New England Aquarium that ran on local television when I was growing up, usually on Saturday mornings when Chris and I would watch wrestling—the WCCW of the Von Erich brothers and the Gentleman Chris Adams, my personal favorite, before it was eclipsed by the WWF.

111 – Emerald Cities

The gangrenous, double-decked, cantilevered bridge

This is the Tobin Bridge, which spans the Mystic River and connects Boston to its northern suburbs via Route 1.

83 – Archaeopteryx

Risotto was the caterer's specialty. I spent hours
in his kitchen on Beacon Street rinsing it from china

This is not the same Beacon Street as in **43 – Nucleus Accumbens**. That Beacon Street is located in Boston proper. This one is located in Somerville. It is a quaint quirk of the road system in Boston and surrounding towns and cities, that they will each have their own versions of the same street name, which is why visitors to Boston love driving here.

51 - Tesseract

the last leg of the bus's route forty years ago.

Visitors to Boston will have noticed that the MBTA system's Green
Line has spurs lettered B, C, D, and E. The extinct line that ran where
the last leg of the 51 bus route now runs was the A train. It split
off from the current B train track at Packard's Corner and ran along
Cambridge Street to Washington Street through Brighton Center and
out to Watertown, a suburb just west of the city.

93 - Fear of Falling

The title of this poem is taken from the book of the same name by
Barbara Ehrenreich, in which she explores the anxieties of America's
middle class during the second half of the 20th century.

15 - I will die in Boston on a Saturday afternoon

The format for this poem was taken from Cesar Vallejo's "Black
Stone Lying On A White Stone" which begins, "I will die in Paris,
on a rainy day." This format has been used by other poets as well,
including Donald Justice, "Variations On A Text By Vallejo," and
Tony Hoagland, "Black SUV: (After Vallejo)."

SL1 - Dun Aengus

Dun is the Irish word for fort.

On black water, the silhouettes of fishing trawlers
bobbed as they have since they were hide-fit curraghs.

Curragh, or currach, is a type of boat used along the west coast of
Ireland for centuries. Their hulls were originally made from the hides
of animal skins, which were stretched over a wooden frame. Today,
they are usually made from canvas.

1 – Voyagers to the West

The title of this poem is taken from a study of American colonial immigration patterns written by the Harvard historian, Bernard Bailyn, who also happened to be one of my professors in college, though he would never remember me as I almost never attended his class. His work, *Voyagers to the West*, was awarded the Pulitzer Prize in 1987.

201 – Imram

Imrams, or imramha, are old Irish tales, usually about great sea journeys. The greatest of those journeys and the greatest of those imramha is the one about Saint Brendan.

The Bus Routes

1   Harvard/Holyoke Gate – Dudley Station via Mass Ave

4   North Station – World Trade Center via Federal Courthouse & South Station

9   City Point – Copley Square via Broadway Station

10 City Point – Copley Square via Andrew Station & BU Medical Center

15 Kane Square or Fields Corner Station – Ruggles Station via Uphams Corner

16 Forest Hills Station – Andrew Station or UMass via Columbia Rd

17 Fields Corner Station – Andrew Station via Uphams Corner & Edward Everett Square

18 Ashmont Station – Andrew Station via Fields Corner Station

28 Mattapan Station – Ruggles Station via Dudley Station

35 Dedham Mall/Stimson St – Forest Hills Station via Belgrade Ave & Centre St

36 Charles River Loop or V.A. Hospital – Forest Hills Station via Belgrade Ave & Centre St

37 Baker & Vermont Sts. – Forest Hills Station via Belgrade Ave & Centre St

39 Forest Hills Station – Back Bay Station via Huntington Ave

43 Ruggles Station – Park & Tremont Sts. via Tremont St

47 Central Square, Cambridge – Broadway Station via BU Medical Center, Dudley Station & Longwood Medical Area

51 Cleveland Circle – Forest Hills Station via Hancock Village

52:71	Dedham Mall or Charles River Loop - Watertown Yard via Oak Hill & Newton Center : Watertown Square - Harvard Station via Mt Auburn St
55	Jersey & Queensberry - Copley Square or Park & Tremont Sts. via Ipswich St
57	Watertown Yard - Kenmore Station via Newton Corner & Brighton Center
60	Chestnut Hill - Kenmore Station via Brookline Village & Cypress St
65	Brighton Center - Kenmore Station via Washington St, Brookline Village & Brookline Ave
83	Rindge Ave - Central Square, Cambridge via Porter Square Station
89	Clarendon Hill or Davis Square - Sullivan Square Station via Broadway
93	Sullivan Square Station - Downtown via Bunker Hill St & Haymarket Station
111	Woodlawn or Broadway & Park Ave - Haymarket Station via Mystic River/Tobin Bridge
201	Fields Corner or North Quincy Station - Fields Corner via Neponset Ave to Adams St
214:216	Quincy Center Station - Germantown via Sea St & O'Brien Towers : Quincy Center Station - Houghs Neck via Sea St
SL1	Logan Airport - South Station via Waterfront
SL5	Dudley Station - Downtown via Washington St

ACKNOWLEDGMENTS

I am grateful to the editors of the publications where these poems first appeared: "1 - Voyagers to the West," "10 - Panopticon," "39 - Communion," "43 - Nucleus Accumbens," "47 - Tattoos," "52:71 - Stage Fright," and "83 - Archaeopteryx" in *apt*; "SL1 - Dun Aengus" in *Slow Trains*; "37 - Guardian Angel" in *U.m.Ph! Prose*; and "9 - Mirror Neurons" in *Wilderness House Literary Review*. I would also like to thank Mary Pinard for selecting "Home Front" and "Pets" as winners in the West Roxbury Branch of the Boston Public Library annual poetry competition. To quote Breaker Morant, "We poets do crave immortality, you know."

I am deeply indebted to Carissa Halston and Randolph Pfaff for their support of this project from the outset. They published the first four poems in the series what seems like a lifetime ago now and have patiently waited for me to complete it so that they could publish it in book form. I am not so foolhardy as to be unable to recognize that this collection never would have appeared without them.

I am also indebted to all of the relatives and friends who, some unbeknownst to them, had such an impact on me and my life that I rendered them in poetry. Though I have not spoken to some of them in years and they are scattered throughout the country, they remain my friends and always will.

Lastly, I must express my sincerest gratitude to my wife, Nicole, who has not only read and commented on practically every draft of every poem contained in the collection, but whose idea for a series of poems about different bus routes it was in the first place. She is a stern, but loving editor and her support means more to me than anything. I could not do what I did without her.

About the Author

Liam Day has been a youth worker, teacher, assistant principal, public health professional, campaign manager, political pundit, communications director, and professional basketball player. His poems have appeared at *Slow Trains*, *apt*, and *Wilderness House Literary Review*. His op-eds and essays have appeared in *Annalemma*, *Stymie*, *The Boston Globe*, *Boston Herald*, and *The Good Men Project*, where he is the Sports Editor.

About the Publisher

Aforementioned Productions is an award-winning small press and 501(c)(3) non-profit organization that publishes chapbooks, full-length collections of prose and poetry, and the weekly online/ annual print literary journal *apt*; and organizes readings, theatrical performances, and other literary events. Founded in 2005 and run by Carissa Halston and Randolph Pfaff, Aforementioned's aesthetic favors challenging writing that combines the cerebral and the visceral.

Aforementioned is supported primarily through book sales and reader contributions. Donations to Aforementioned are tax-deductible.

To make a donation, visit aforementioned.org/donate.